The Medal of Honor

CORNERSTONES OF FREEDOM™

SECOND SERIES

Roger Wachtel

Children's Press®
A Division of Scholastic Inc.
New York • Toronto • London • Auckland • Sydney
Mexico City • New Delhi • Hong Kong
Danbury, Connecticut

Photographs © 2002: AP/Wide World Photos: 34, 45 bottom right (J. Scott Applewhite), 40, 41 (Charlie Riedel), 32; Archive Photos/Getty Images: 36 (RDA), 26 (Earl Young), 20; Congressional Medal of Honor Society, Mt. Pleasant, SC: 5, 10, 16, 45 left; Corbis Images: 3, 4 bottom, 23, 25 (Bettmann), 14 (Mathew Brady), 18 (Francis G. Mayer), 39 (Peter Turnley), cover background, 8 bottom, 24; Hulton|Archive/Getty Images: 22 (American Stock), 15, 27, 28, 44 bottom; Liberty Memorial Museum, Kansas City, MO: cover bottom right, cover top left, 6, 19, 21, 37, 38; North Wind Picture Archives: 8 top (N. Carter), 7, 9, 12, 44 top; Stock Montage, Inc.: 4 top, 13, 17, 44 left; The Image Works: 33, 45 top (Mark Reinstein), 11, 29 (Joe Sohm); U.S. Central Intelligence Agency/Texas A&M University Libraries: 35; U.S. Navy photograph: 31.

Library of Congress Cataloging-in-Publication Data
Wachtel, Roger.
   The Medal of Honor / Roger Wachtel.
      p. cm.—(Cornerstones of freedom)
   Includes bibliographical references and index.
   ISBN 0-516-22265-1
   1. Medal of Honor—Juvenile literature. 2. United States—Armed
Forces—Biography—Juvenile literature. [1. Medal of Honor. 2. United
States—Armed Forces—Biography.] I. Title. II. Series.

UB433 .W33 2002
355.1'342—dc21

                              00-060248

1 2 3 4 5 6 7 8 9 10 R 11 10 09 08 07 06 05 04 03 02

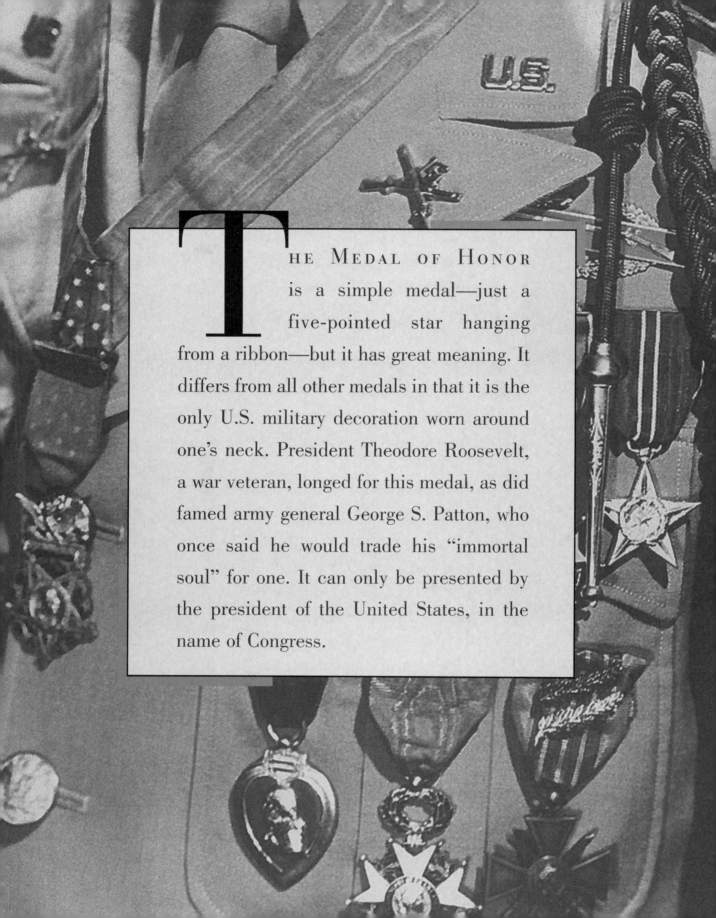

THE MEDAL OF HONOR is a simple medal—just a five-pointed star hanging from a ribbon—but it has great meaning. It differs from all other medals in that it is the only U.S. military decoration worn around one's neck. President Theodore Roosevelt, a war veteran, longed for this medal, as did famed army general George S. Patton, who once said he would trade his "immortal soul" for one. It can only be presented by the president of the United States, in the name of Congress.

President Theodore Roosevelt served during the Spanish American War but did not receive a Medal of Honor.

ULTIMATE BRAVERY

The **recipients** of the Medal of Honor are rarely famous, even though the medal represents the highest honor a member of the U.S. military can receive. When Congress first authorized the medal, it was to be given to a person who ". . .in action involving actual conflict with an enemy, distinguishes himself **conspicuously** by **gallantry** and **intrepidity** at the risk of his life above and beyond the call of duty." It only goes to the bravest of the brave, and so it is aptly called the Medal of Honor.

Over the years, a few misconceptions have arisen about the Medal of Honor. First, even though it is commonly called the Congressional Medal of Honor, its correct name is simply the Medal of Honor. Second, the soldiers, sailors, marines, and airmen who wear them should not be described as "winners," but rather as "recipients." Medals are often awarded for actions that occurred in the face of great violence and death. Many servicemen died performing their act of bravery. It is for such reasons that "recipients" seems to be a more appropriate term than "winners."

Famous World War II General George S. Patton never received the Medal of Honor.

The Army Medal of Honor

Yet, those servicemen who have them are winners in many ways. Medal of Honor recipients can be characterized as honest, giving, dedicated, and devoted. Humility seems to be their most common attribute. They recognize that there are many acts of bravery in war that go unnoticed. They were simply lucky, many will tell you, to have been singled out to represent thousands of courageous servicemen who were equally deserving of the Medal of Honor. This feeling was best expressed by Major Jay

Zeamer, Jr., a World War II pilot with the U.S. Army Air Corps who received his medal for actions in the Solomon Islands. Zeamer was shot twice and suffered a broken leg, but he continued to fly. He fought off enemy aircraft for forty minutes, shooting down five of them. Then he safely returned his aircraft to its base 500 miles (805 kilometers) away. "For every Medal of Honor awarded," he reflects, "there are many instances of heroism not observed, or not reported or not written up. Whenever I wear my medal, I can't help thinking of those men and considering my medal as representative and symbolic of them, they who received no recognition except, in some cases, a **posthumous** Purple Heart."

FAMILY OF HONOR

Five sets of brothers, but only one father-son combination, have received medals. Lt. Arthur MacArthur received his medal for Civil War action. His son, General Douglas MacArthur, was honored for a distinguished military career when he was sixty-two, which also made him the oldest recipient of the medal.

The Purple Heart was established by George Washington for soldiers wounded in battle.

This map shows the division of North and South in the United States in 1861.

THE FIRST MEDALS

Today, the award goes only to servicemen who perform the bravest acts, but it hasn't always been so. The Medal of Honor has its origin in the U.S. Civil War. In 1861 many of the Southern states **seceded** from the Union and formed their own country. Before long, the army of the Confederate States of America fired on U.S. troops, and these two countries, once one nation, were at war.

The Confederate flag, the symbol of the South during the Civil War

★ ★ ★ ★

The war that ended slavery was extraordinarily destructive. Eventually, 620,000 soldiers died and countless others were wounded, many crippled for life. Some wounds caused a very slow and painful death. In addition, whole towns were wiped out. The method of warfare also caused an immense number of men to die. Massed "charges" into heavily defended enemy positions could result in thousands of deaths in a matter of minutes. Even worse, the soldiers were fighting their former countrymen, and so they sometimes fought against relatives, friends, and even brothers. People remained angry about the issues of the war for decades.

Wounded Civil War soldiers being cared for by nurse Anne Bell

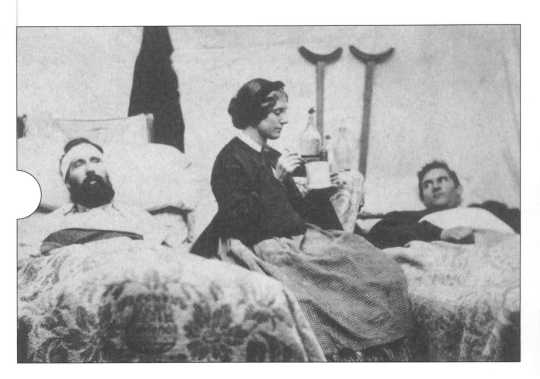

Slavery was one of the issues that led to the Civil War.

Many Civil War soldiers were poorly educated and didn't really understand the complex issues of the war. They often joined the army for the adventure of it. They had no idea what they were getting themselves into, and many of them deserted when they saw what war was really like.

Word of mass **desertions** quickly spread to Washington, and congressmen worried about keeping the army together. They therefore began creating awards to help the men's **morale**. If soldiers distinguished themselves in battle, Congress would give them a medal. In 1861 and 1862, first

An old version of the Army Medal of Honor

NATIONAL MEDAL OF HONOR DAY

On March 25, 1863, the first medals were awarded. They went to ten from the group of nineteen Civil War Union spies known as Andrews' Raiders, who cut off a Confederate supply line on April 12, 1862. Four of the Raiders to receive awards were already dead, so this also marks the first posthumous medals.

the navy and then the army created medals of honor. These medals recognized those who acted with bravery and were the forerunners of today's Medal of Honor.

The earliest act of heroism that resulted in the awarding of a Medal of Honor took place far from Civil War battlefields. In 1861, Bernard J.D. Irwin was serving as an assistant surgeon in the **Arizona Territory** at Fort Buchanan where the U.S. Army was doing battle with Apache warriors. Although Irwin was a doctor, not a soldier, when he got word that sixty U.S. troops were surrounded and

✦ ✦ ✦ ✦

outmanned, he decided to do something. He and the fourteen soldiers left in the fort rode mules 100 miles (160 km) through a blizzard to the site of the battle. Irwin then carefully placed the men to make them appear to be a much larger force than they actually were. His trick worked. The warriors thought they were outnumbered, and all sixty soldiers were rescued. It would be thirty-three years before Irwin would be recognized, but this was the first heroic act for which the Medal of Honor was awarded.

The Civil War produced many Medal of Honor recipients. The earliest were the survivors of a sabotage team known as Andrews' Raiders, led by James J. Andrews. In 1862, they stole a locomotive near Marietta, Georgia, in an attempt to destroy the railroad lines that were used to

Railroad lines were valuable modes of transportation of supplies during the Civil War.

supply Confederate troops. Some of Andrews' Raiders were killed, and others were captured and hanged as spies. Actions in which men put their lives on the line for their country occurred frequently and these men were often rewarded with a Medal of Honor.

ONLY FOR THE MOST DESERVING

In the Civil War, there was also a great deal of hand-to-hand combat—fierce, close fighting that produced many heroes. As the war progressed, however, many less heroic acts began to be recognized as well. One such instance involved the awarding of Medals of Honor to hundreds of soldiers for extending

A painting of the Confederate charge up Little Round Top during the Battle of Gettysburg

their enlistment by four days to defend Washington, D.C. In 1863 the U.S. government, worried that if the Confederates won at Gettysburg they would march on Washington next, asked the soldiers to defend the capital. This was an important safety precaution, but the soldiers never saw battle, and their actions could not be considered heroic.

The Medal of Honor was further cheapened when many soldiers who had not distinguished themselves in battle decided they would like to have one, too. They persuaded their congressmen, who saw it as a great way to get votes, to sponsor them. In effect, the soldiers nominated themselves. This action angered those who had truly gone above and beyond the call of duty, and the military leadership decided that the rules for getting a medal would have to be toughened. First, it was ruled that soldiers could no longer nominate themselves. Then in 1917, President Woodrow Wilson convened a board of generals to review all past Medals of Honor. This board revoked many of the medals that had been given for lesser actions, in particular, the awards that

DOUBLE RECIPIENTS

People often wonder why there are more medals given than individual recipients. Fourteen men have received two Medals of Honor for two separate acts of bravery. Civil War sailor John Cooper received his first in 1864 for staying at his post and working his gun with skill under tremendous fire in Mobile Bay. Almost a year later, he rescued a crewmate from an exploding ammunition locker, gaining a rare second citation.

President Woodrow Wilson

were made to the soldiers who defended Washington, D.C., in 1863. This action of the board temporarily stripped the medal from Dr. Mary Edwards Walker, one of history's most unusual recipients. She was not only one of the few nonmilitary awardees but also the only woman ever to receive the Medal of Honor.

AN UNUSUAL RECIPIENT

Dr. Mary Edwards Walker was one of the few female surgeons in the country when the Civil War broke out, and she felt it was her duty to serve her country. When the army rejected her, she refused to take no for an answer.

Dr. Mary Edwards Walker, surgeon during the Civil War

She went to work first in the army hospital in Washington, D.C., and then in the Union **encampment** in Warrenton, Virginia. She hoped that when the army saw her work it would see she was an excellent surgeon and would accept her services. When she arrived, however, a **typhoid** epidemic had broken out. The army needed every doctor it could get, regardless of gender. Walker's career as a soldier's doctor had begun.

She served well and earned the respect of her superiors. In 1864, Dr. Walker applied to be a civilian surgeon for the 52nd Ohio Volunteers, but the rules said she had to submit to an examination by a medical review board. Her skills were excellent, but the board rejected her anyway, probably because she was a woman. The medical panel

YOUNG AND BRAVE

The youngest recipient of the Medal of Honor was Civil War soldier Willie Johnston, who was thirteen when he received the Medal for being the only drummer boy to hold on to his instrument during a retreat where strong, full-grown soldiers threw away their equipment so there would be less weight to carry. The twentieth century's youngest recipient was Jack Lucas, who threw himself on a **grenade** during World War II when he was just seventeen, his third year in the Marines!

Willie Johnston—the Civil War's youngest Medal of Honor recipient

ridiculed her medical skills as those of a "housewife." It was also shocked that she wore men's clothing. Not only did women's clothes, with their tight waists, appear to be unhealthy to Dr. Walker, but she also had seen how the nurses had to wring the blood from their long skirts while working in the army hospitals. So it just made more sense to her to wear men's clothes. The conservative panel, however, thought that was inappropriate.

Nonetheless, the leadership of the 52nd Ohio ignored the medical panel and, recognizing Dr. Walker's skills, let her continue to work. She treated soldiers, tended to the injured behind enemy lines, and even delivered letters to soldiers. Captured as a spy while delivering these letters, she was placed in a prison camp. In the course of caring for the other prisoners, she became ill. That illness cost her the ability to practice medicine.

In 1865 President Lincoln, ignoring the fact that Dr. Walker had never been commissioned, awarded her the Medal anyway in recognition of her "services and sufferings." Dr. Walker wore her medal proudly, even after the panel revoked it, until her death in 1919. When her medal was finally restored in 1977, a new tombstone and bronze plaque were erected to recognize her service to a country that officially refused to accept her but was forever in her debt.

President Abraham Lincoln

OLD AND NEW

OLD AND NEW

In the early 1900s, the Medal was redesigned. Recipients were given new ones, but many of them refused to give up their original ones. It was decided that they could keep both but could only wear one at a time.

George Washington established the first U.S. medal for gallantry.

MORE MEDALS FOR BRAVERY

For several years after 1917, the Medal of Honor was almost constantly reassessed, and it became more difficult to receive one. In the Civil War, for instance, 1,520 Medals of Honor were awarded. In contrast, only 440 were given during World War II, and 131 during the Korean War. In the Vietnam War, the number of recipients totaled only 239, despite the fact that it was a very long war. There were just as many brave soldiers, but now the government considered only the highest acts of **valor.**

As these changes occurred, however, the government faced a new problem. While it had significantly increased the requirements for the medal, there were still difficult wars to be fought, and all kinds of heroism had to be recognized. The solution was to establish a system of awards in which lesser acts of heroism and long terms of distinguished service were also recognized. Some, such as the Soldier's Medal, even rewarded bravery and heroism during times of peace. The government also instituted many additional medals for bravery in combat.

One of the medals that a soldier can earn is the Badge of Military Merit, now known as the Purple Heart. It was a medal that had been established by George Washington on August 7, 1782, but it had fallen into disuse shortly thereafter. The government decided to begin awarding it again in 1932 to recognize soldiers who had been wounded in battle. Another medal is the Silver Star, which rewards heroism in battle that doesn't quite meet Medal of Honor standards.

The U.S. Silver Star, established July 9, 1918, is given for acts of bravery that are of a lesser degree than acts that would warrant a Distinguished Service Cross.

Sergeant Alvin C. York, shown wearing his medals

THE QUIET HERO

Most Medal recipients return to ordinary lives. A few, however, have become very famous as a result of their heroism. One of these is known to millions simply as Sergeant York.

Alvin C. York was a backwoods Tennessean whose life in the hills, hunting from a very young age, helped him become one of the greatest marksmen in World War I. When

20

he was called to duty, he was reluctant to serve. Not only was he unsure of the morality of taking human life, but his mother depended on him and he was devoted to her. Like millions of others, however, he answered his country's call. Ultimately, he would perform one of the most remarkable feats in the history of warfare.

In October 1918, York, then a corporal, was with a patrol of seventeen men sent to wipe out German machine guns on a hill in France. Their simple rifles were no match for the weapons of the enemy, and in a short time York's patrol was pinned down by the enemy's rapid-fire guns. The Germans on the hill, spotting the patrol in a clearing, started shooting the machine guns. York and his fellow soldiers were in great danger, and York knew he had to act.

Armed with just a pistol and a rifle, York took the few men who were not wounded or killed and moved toward the enemy. He crept to within 40 yards (36.6 meters) of the enemy position. Using only a bush for cover and his uncanny ability as a crack shot, he engaged the Germans. First, he began picking off the machine gunners one by one. Then, he killed seven soldiers as they charged him with fixed **bayonets**. He went back to shooting machine gunners, calling to them to surrender so he wouldn't have to kill any more, and eventually

The Distinguished Service Cross, established July 9, 1918, is awarded for acts of bravery that do not hold Medal of Honor status.

they did. When the Germans threw down their ammunition and gave up, they were amazed to see that just one man had done almost all of the damage.

York's superiors were every bit as amazed to find that he had killed twenty Germans, disabled thirty-five machine guns, and captured 132 prisoners all by himself. His only comment on his actions was that while he hadn't wanted to kill anyone, the enemy had left him no choice. It was either kill them or let his men die.

Corporal York was promoted to sergeant and was awarded the Distinguished Service Cross and the Medal of Honor, as well as many medals from countries that were allied with the United States. He returned to the United States as one of the most famous men in the world. He was honored in

From left to right: George Tobias, Gary Cooper (playing Sergeant York), and Joe Sawyer in director Howard Hawks's film *Sergeant York*

ARMY COURAGE

Of all of the branches of the U.S. armed forces, the army has received the most Medals, almost three times as many as the navy, which has received the second most. The marines and the air force rank in third and fourth. Douglas Munro is the only member of the U.S. Coast Guard to receive a medal. In 1942, under constant fire, he led a group of five small boats to rescue marines from Guadalcanal. Munro purposely put his boat directly in the line of fire to shield the other boats during the rescue, giving up his own life to save five hundred others.

**World War II hero
Audie Murphy**

New York with a ticker tape parade and was offered huge sums of money for the right to tell his story. A movie was even made about his life.

AMERICA'S MOST DECORATED

World War II's best-known hero was Audie Murphy, who became so famous that he actually became a movie star. Murphy came from a very poor home, and thinking that a soldier's pay would help his family, he enlisted in the army at the age of eighteen. At that age, he had to have his mother's consent to join.

★ ★ ★ ★

He started as a private but soon rose to the rank of sergeant and eventually received a field commission as a second lieutenant. He fought in nine major campaigns, was wounded three times, and he killed more than 240 of the enemy. He eventually received thirty-three awards and medals, including five from France and Belgium, which made him the most decorated soldier in World War II.

It is said that Murphy earned the Medal of Honor many times over, but it was his performance in France in 1945 that was most responsible for his honor. While he was in command of an infantry company, Murphy's men were attacked by waves of a superior enemy force and six tanks. The enemy's guns hit a nearby vehicle, setting it on fire. Its crew ran for cover, but Murphy jumped on top of it, ignoring the fact that it could explode at any minute. He began using its machine gun against the Germans. Murphy was alone and unprotected, with dozens of enemy soldiers and six tanks bearing down on him, but he held his ground. He fought that way for an hour, displaying incredible courage. He killed dozens of enemy soldiers and forced the tanks to fall back. He was shot in the leg but ignored his wound. The men and tanks got to within ten yards of Murphy, but he pushed them back. Finally he ran out of ammunition, and gave up his position.

Then he went back to the woods for help. Refusing medical attention, he rallied his troops and organized a counterattack that won the battle. When it was all over, he had killed fifty of the enemy and saved his own men from being slaughtered.

General Alexander Patch decorates Lt. Audie Murphy with the Medal of Honor.

Not all of the medal recipients are known by name. Several medals have been awarded to unknown soldiers. Some of the American unknowns are buried in graves honored with a permanent guard at Arlington National Cemetery. Five soldiers of important U.S. allies have also recieved Medals of honor.

What Murphy might have been feeling in those moments was voiced by another Medal of Honor recipient, Gino Merli. Merli was an army machine gunner who received his medal for action near Sars la Bruyere, Belgium, in 1945. He was under extremely heavy fire and was actually overrun by the enemy several times. Each time they got to him, however, he pretended to be dead. The enemy would leave and he would begin firing again. Amazingly, this unusual tactic resulted in fifty-two enemy kills and the surrender of German troops. Years later, he reflected on what makes a soldier perform such extreme acts of courage. "You are no longer a person. . . . You think, 'My new family, the men I came with, are dying . . . help them . . . get rid of those who are trying to kill them. Make this stop. Make this stop."

A guard keeps constant watch over the Tomb of the Unknown Soldier at Arlington National Cemetery.

Like Sergeant York before him, Audie Murphy returned to the United States a famous hero. He became a Hollywood actor, even playing himself on the screen in the story of his life, *To Hell and Back*. He made fifty films and was a successful songwriter.

Audie Murphy's life wasn't the same after the war, however. He suffered from what was then called "battle fatigue" but is now known as post-traumatic stress disorder (PTSD). This is a type of emotional distress caused by

exposure to the horrors of battle. It can cause nightmares and sometimes **hallucinations** of battle action. At the time, few soldiers talked about it because they thought it was a sign of cowardice. Eventually, Murphy let it be known that he suffered from it and used his fame to force the government to recognize the disorder and treat veterans who were afflicted by it. Today PTSD is recognized as a common byproduct of war.

Audie Murphy died in a plane crash in 1971, at the age of forty-six, and was buried with all the honors befitting a war hero in Arlington National Cemetery near Washington, D.C. His grave is one of the most visited in Arlington, second only to President John F. Kennedy's.

Arlington National cemetary, where many American heroes are buried

★ ★ ★ ★

THE ULTIMATE SACRIFICE

Military cemeteries like Arlington are filled with men who gave their lives in battle. When he dedicated the military cemetery at Gettysburg, President Abraham Lincoln stated that giving one's life for his country is the ultimate sacrifice. He called it "the last full measure of devotion." Not surprisingly, many Medal of Honor recipients are men who died in the service of their country. One such soldier is Army Corporal Mitchell Red Cloud, Jr.

Corporal Red Cloud was serving in the Korean War on November 5, 1950. Standing in front of his fellow soldiers on a ridge, he saw Chinese Communist soldiers charging their posi-

Korean War Medal of Honor recipient Corporal Mitchell Red Cloud, Jr.

tion. He stood and fired into the advancing army, slowing their advance. He held his position until he was severely wounded. Despite his injuries, he refused medical aid, wrapping his arm around a tree for support. He kept firing until he was fatally wounded.

This most heroic act slowed the enemy advance enough to allow Corporal Red Cloud's company to organize its defense and to remove wounded soldiers. Corporal Red Cloud saved numerous lives through his incredible self-sacrifice. It is

THE HERO SAVES A HERO

On Halloween night in Vietnam in 1972, Michael Thornton risked his life to save Thomas R. Norris. Thornton received word during a mission that Norris, his leader, had been mortally wounded. Under intense gunfire he rushed to Norris's last position and killed two enemy who were about to overtake it. Thornton found Norris badly wounded, but alive. He inflated Norris' life jacket and towed him toward the sea until they were picked up by the support craft. Norris had already been nominated for a Medal of Honor, so this marks the only known time that a medal was awarded to a person for saving another medal recipient.

Vietnam Medal of Honor recipient Michael Thornton

an act that will never be forgotten by those who were there or by the U.S. military, which has named both an army camp and a naval ship for him.

WHAT IS A HERO?

Of course, there are many kinds of heroism. Like Audie Murphy before him, Bob Kerrey used his notoriety to force the country to face a difficult issue and one of the most unpleasant aspects of war.

Lieutenant Kerrey was leader of a Navy SEAL (Sea, Air, and Land) team during the Vietnam War. The SEALs, an elite military force trained in every aspect of combat, often parachute into the ocean in **SCUBA** gear, then swim to their land objective behind enemy lines. They are among the most highly trained men in the military.

Kerrey led his team on a very important mission near Nha Trang Bay, Republic of Vietnam, on March 14, 1969. They were to capture important enemy officers to gain information that would save American lives. After scaling a 350-foot cliff, the team split into two units. Suddenly it was attacked by the enemy. A grenade exploded at Kerrey's feet. He was thrown back onto jagged rocks and was badly wounded. Although he was bleeding badly from wounds that would eventually cost him one of his legs, he thought only of his men and the mission.

Unable to move and fighting unconsciousness, he calmly directed the teams by radio and caught the enemy in a crossfire. He remained cool and directed the capture of enemy soldiers; then he called in helicopters to evacuate the area. Not only did his actions save his own men, but the information obtained from the enemy saved countless others.

Back in the States after the war, Kerrey first became a successful businessman and then the governor of, and finally senator from, Nebraska. As he prepared to retire, however, he called a press conference. He discussed how uncomfortable the title "hero" had always made him. This was especially true, he explained, because he had participated in military actions that had resulted in the death of civilians.

Senator Bob Kerrey

Kerrey's admission was a very difficult reminder of one of the most terrible costs of war. It was particularly startling coming from a man who had been in the public eye for so long—especially so for a Medal of Honor recipient. It would be naïve to believe that only soldiers die in war, but civilian casualties are often ignored in history books. It was obviously hard for Kerrey to discuss something he had carried with him for so long, but it was also very important. This recipient reminded us that there is very little glory when people die.

IT'S NEVER TOO LATE TO HONOR A HERO

The Medal of Honor is such an important means of recognizing the sacrifice of members of the armed forces that many people work for years to have a comrade recognized for an act of bravery. A situation of this type resulted in one of the most recent Medal of Honor recipients.

Alfred Rascon was born in Mexico. He wasn't even a citizen of the United States when he volunteered to serve in the Vietnam War out of love for his adopted country. He was trained as a medic, and in 1966 he risked his life to help his fellow soldiers.

Alfred Rascon receives his Medal of Honor from President Bill Clinton.

Vietnam is a country in southeast Asia. The capitol is Hanoi and the largest city is Ho Chi Minh City, formerly Saigon.

In Vietnam on March 16, 1966, his platoon was under attack, and his men were hurt. Rascon ran to the wounded. Exposed, he was hit multiple times by **shrapnel**. Even when a grenade exploded in his face, he still performed his duties, treating wounds and delivering ammunition to a machine gunner. He covered the wounded with his body as he treated them.

Two of the men he saved recommended him for the medal, but the paperwork was lost. He received the Silver Star instead, but nothing less than the nation's highest honor was appropriate. One of the men saved, Ray Compton, said, "Neither of us would be here if it weren't for Al. Maybe not in his own eyes, but in our eyes he's a hero. No doubt about it." They finally had their request hand

35

Grenade explosions were one of many hazards faced by soldiers in Vietnam.

delivered to the president and secretary of defense, and on February 8, 2000, Alfred Rascon received his Medal of Honor.

Nearly 3,500 men and one woman have received the Medal of Honor. They have acted as few of us can, risking their own lives for those of their comrades. It is an honor for a very rare action. Men who wear them do so proudly and often talk of other men who performed ultimate acts of courage but were not recognized.

There are as many reasons for awarding the Medal of Honor as there are soldiers, sailors, and airmen who have received it. But what separates a brave act from one worthy of this ultimate reward? Two of the most recent recipients,

Sergeants Gary Gordon and Randall Shughart, demonstrate the difference perfectly. Not only did they give their lives to save a fellow soldier, but they practically had to beg for permission to do so.

In the early 1990's, people in the African country of Somalia were suffering through very bad times. Millions were starving and powerful criminals called warlords were stealing food meant for the poor. They then either kept it for themselves, or sold it for profit. Innocent people were dying, so the U.S. military was sent in to stop the abuse.

In early October 1993, a raid on one of the warlords met more resistance than was expected. Rockets were fired at the soldiers and their helicopter crashed. The badly injured pilot and crew were surrounded by armed and hostile crowds. Gary Gordon and Randall Shughart, members of the elite Army Rangers, were on another helicopter flying overhead and could see that the crewmen had no chance of survival unless someone was on the ground to help. Unfortunately, the ground was a very dangerous place.

The Rangers believe in the idea that "I will not fail those with whom I serve," and Gordon and Shughart were clearly acting on that belief. While they probably felt that they could successfully defend themselves, they also understood that there was a good chance they would die if they went in to help. They planned to hold off the enemy until ground troops could get there, but even their own pilot said no one in their right mind would do it. Their commander obviously felt that way as well. When they asked permission to land and protect the injured they were denied. It was simply too dangerous to risk it.

World War I soldier Waldo Hatler, wearing the version of the Medal of Honor that is worn around the neck

★ ★ ★ ★

FOR MOM

Only one woman has received a Medal of
Honor, but two are inscribed with women's
names. Capt. Jay Vargas claimed his mother,
who had just died, was the source of his
bravery, so her name, M. Sando Vargas,
is on his Medal.

World War I Medal of Honor
recipient John Lewis Barkley
wears his medal—among
others—pinned to
his uniform.

The Rangers have a motto: "Leave no man
behind." So, Gordon again requested permission to
land, and again was denied. Finally on the third try,
they were allowed to go in. Since there was too much
debris at the crash site and too many armed and hostile Somalis on the ground, they slid down ropes from
the helicopter to the ground 100 yards away from the
downed helicopter. Armed only with pistols and their
sniper rifles, Gordon and Shughart fought their way
through dense fire to the crash site.

They pulled the pilot and crew from the damaged helicopter and set up a defensive position. They were under
heavy fire and were very vulnerable to attack. When their
ammunition was depleted, they went back to the
wreck for more. Soon Shughart was fatally
wounded. Gordon took his own rifle with its last
five rounds to Michael Durant, the injured pilot,
handed it to him, and said, "Good luck." Armed
only with his pistol, he went back into the firefight and was soon killed. However, the pilot
survived. "Without a doubt," Durant says, "I
owe my life to these two men and their bravery."

Why did these men do what they did? Many
like Audie Murphy, Alvin York, and Alfred
Rascon did it to keep their men alive. Not too
long ago, Joseph J. McCarthy, who received
his Medal of Honor for action in World War II,
summed up this feeling perfectly, saying, "I
had a stroke a few months ago, and I

38

A group of starving people in Somalia gather for food.

have a little trouble talking and writing sometimes, but I don't have any trouble remembering my boys. I can still see their faces, all those brave boys. Doesn't matter how many years go by, I can still see them all—and I know what they gave for their country. I love them all."

The actions of Medal of Honor recipients are acts of devotion, to the mission, to the country, to one another—their friends, their "new family." In the eyes of those who receive it, the Medal of Honor isn't about acts of bravery at all; it is about acts of love.

Roger Donlon displays his Medal of Honor in front of a painting depicting the Vietnam battle for which he was awarded the medal.

41

Glossary

Arizona Territory—area in American Southwest before states in that area had been established

bayonets—blades adapted to fit on the muzzles of rifles

civilian—one who is not in the military

conspicuously—acting in a way that attracts attention

desertions—abandoning one's military duty illegally

encampment—a base for military personnel

gallantry—courage

grenade—a small bomb, usually thrown and designed to break apart

hallucinations—visions of something that appears real but is imaginary

intrepidity—fearlessness

morale—the mental attitude of a group

posthumous—occurring after someone's death

recipients—people who receive or are given possession
of something

scouts—soldiers who are sent to a forward position
to get information

SCUBA—acronym for Self-Contained Underwater
Breathing Apparatus; refers to equipment used
to explore underwater

seceded—formally withdrew from a group

shrapnel—metal fragments from an explosion

typhoid—a highly contagious, sometimes deadly, disease
that causes high fever and other symptoms

valor—personal bravery

Timeline: The Medal of

1861

FEBRUARY 13
Army Assistant Surgeon Bernard J.D. Irwin performs the first actions that in 1894 were recognized with a Medal of Honor.

JUNE 26
John Williams refuses to leave any man behind on his damaged ship and becomes the first member of the Navy to earn the Medal of Honor.

DECEMBER 21
President Abraham Lincoln signs the order for the first 200 Navy Medals of Honor.

1862

FEBRUARY 17
Congress authorizes the Army Medal of Honor.

• • • • • • • • •

MAY 12
Corporal John Mackie becomes the first Marine Medal of Honor recipient.

• • • • • • • •

JUNE 18
Seven of Andrews' Raiders are hanged as spies in Atlanta.

JULY 12
President Lincoln signs the order to prepare 2,000 Medals of Honor. They are only for enlisted men. To this date, 88 men had performed actions that would earn them Medals.

1863

MARCH 3
Legislation extends medals to officers as well as enlisted men.

• • • • • • • • •

MARCH 25
The first Medal of Honor ceremony takes place. Six survivors of Andrews' Raiders receive the Medal.

• • • • • • • •

APRIL 3
The first Navy Medal of Honor is awarded.

MAY 22
Ninety-six soldiers perform Medal of Honor actions in the Battle of Vicksburg. This is the highest one-day total in history.

JULY 1
The Battle of Gettysburg begins. Fifty-eight soldiers earn medals for their actions in the three days of battle.

• • • • • • • • •

JULY 18
Former slave William Harvey Carney becomes the first African American to earn a Medal of Honor.

Honor

1917 | 1919 | 1943 | 1945 | 1969 | 1993 | 2000

FEBRUARY 5
A review board officially revokes 911 Medals of Honor.

MAY 3
Sergeant Alvin C. York receives his Medal of Honor. His actions and fame add to its legendary status.

MAY 23
Private Joseph Martinez is the first Hispanic American to receive a Medal of Honor.

NOVEMBER 10
Football star Captain Maurice "Footsie" Britt becomes the first soldier to earn the Distinguished Service Cross, Silver Star, and Medal of Honor in the same war.

APRIL 5
Private First Class Sadao S. Munemori is the first Japanese American to receive a Medal in World War II. No other Japanese American would be recognized until 2000, when President Clinton awarded the medal to twenty-two Japanese Americans for heroic actions during the war.

MARCH 14
Lieutenant Bob Kerrey earns his Medal of Honor.

OCTOBER 3
Gary Gordon and Randall Shughart, both Army Rangers, are killed performing a rescue mission in Somalia. It is the most recent Medal of Honor action.

FEBRUARY 8
Vietnam War medic Alfred Rascon receives his Medal of Honor for action in Vietnam.

45

To Find Out More

BOOKS

Lemon, Peter C. *Beyond the Medal: From Their Heart to Yours.* Golden, CO: Fulcrum Publishing, 1997.

Kieran Doherty. *Congressional Medal of Honor Recipients.* Berkeley Heights, NJ: Enslow, 1998.

Tom Cassalini, et al. *Ordinary Heroes.* Zionsville, IN: Sweet Pea Press, 2001.

ONLINE SITES

The Congressional Medal of Honor Society
http://www.cmohs.org/

U.S. Army Center of Military History
http://www.army.mil/cmh-pg/moh1.htm

Medal of Honor Museum, Chattanooga, TN
http://www.ngeorgia.com/tenn/mohm.html

Index

Bold numbers indicate illustrations.

About the Author

Roger Wachtel has been an educator for sixteen years, first as a high school English teacher and then as a university instructor. He is now the writing specialist for Peru Community Schools in Peru, Indiana. He was born in New Jersey, went to high school in Belgium, and lives in Westfield, Indiana, with his wife, Jeanette, and three sons, Thomas, Ben, and Josh. He has a Master's degree in English education from Butler University. In his spare time, he reads and writes, follows the New York Mets passionately, and goes to automobile races with his sons and brothers.